THE
DON'T TOUCH
GARDEN

Kate Foley

ARACHNE PRESS

First published in UK 2015 by Arachne Press Limited
100 Grierson Road, London SE23 1NX
www.arachnepress.com
© Arachne Press 2015
ISBN: 978-1-909208-19-3

The moral rights of the author have been asserted
All content is copyright the author.

All rights reserved. This book is sold subject to the condition that it shall not by way of trade or otherwise, be lent, resold, hired out or otherwise circulated without the publisher's prior written consent in any form or binding or cover other than that in which it is published and without similar condition including this condition being imposed on the subsequent purchaser.
Except for short passages for review purposes no part of this publication may be reproduced, stored in a retrieval system or transmitted in any form, or by any means, electronic, mechanical, photocopying, recording or otherwise without prior written permission of Arachne Press.

Poems collected here previously appeared in
Soft Engineering Onlywomen Press, 1994
A Year Without Apricots Blackwater Press, 1999
Night and Other Animals Green Lantern Press, 2002
Laughter from the Hive Shoestring Press, 2004
Cracking On Grey Hen Press 2009
One Window North Shoestring Press, 2012
Quotation page 4 from *Flare in the Leaf and the Cloud* by Mary Oliver, Da Capo Press 2000 by permission.

Printed on wood-free paper in the UK by TJ International, Padstow.

CONTENTS

Introduction	5
Blue Glass Empty Pram	7
Lost Property	8
Well, Daughter...	10
The French for Midwife	12
Adoption	14
The Don't Touch Garden	16
Milk	32
Elephant Aunts	34
The Man on a Bike	36
Mothers and Fathers	39
The Cot of my Bones our Bed	40
Corchipoo	42
Thyrotoxicosis	45
My Father, Counting Sheep	46
Sometimes I Feel Another Face	48
Making the Days	50
The End of a Long Conversation has Come	52
Oral History	54
On Growing a Face	55
The Right Bones	56
Oma	58
Bison	60
Paradox	61

For all my families
and especially my memory bank,
Cousin Nancy

Introduction

'Mirror, mirror on the wall'
the old joke says
'I am my mother after all'

but which?

1938: 4th May: *Thank you for your kind donation of two and sixpence...*

19th August: *I have pleasure in sending you particulars of a dear little girl...*

24th August: *I am so glad to know you are interested in this little Catholic baby and can come on September 5th.*

It will be quite in order for you to take baby if you like her and there is no need to bring any clothing, as baby will be dressed ready for the journey and a small parcel of clothes will be given you at the interview.

So the adoption society wrote in that part of the story, which was of course not only mine, but was where I first appeared.

This was all the introduction my parents had to the complex task of adopting. Their qualification for the job had been a letter from the parish priest saying they were of good character. Since of the only two possible religious options my father recognised – Catholic or lapsed – his was the second, I've wondered, if he'd had to bribe the Father with a bottle of whiskey.

So began the long intertwining of roots which is just as formative as the tangle of parental DNA we are born with.

'What are you going to do when you grow up?' asked my Aunty Margaret. 'Starve in a garret,' I said.

I knew from somewhere that this was an essential hallmark of the writer. My mother's speaking eyebrows nearly climbed off her forehead but it was she who, with the unceasing leaf litter of her stories about her thirteen siblings, taught me the arc of narrative.

Much later, I realised that it was time to move the great ice-age-erratic boulder of secrecy. Still not able to speak face-to-face, I wrote to my parents telling them that I knew. My father replied tenderly, blaming himself – 'I thought not telling was for the best... when we got your letter your mother threw her apron over her head and cried all day.' Old as the walls of Troy, that gesture says it all.

Near the end of her life I was waiting for an ambulance to take my mother, who had finally become too ill for me to nurse in her own home, to the hospice and I began to cry. 'Don't cry,' she whispered. 'O my lovely daughter.'

Sixty years on from that note from the society I found myself standing with my newly discovered brother by the bronze plaque commemorating our biological mother in a San Francisco graveyard, another twist in a narrative which revealed an absent mother but a living family.

This is not the whole of my story any more than anyone's experience of adoption is the whole of theirs. The poet Mary Oliver says in a poem about her parents which is both tender and sad:

'...I will not give them the kiss of complicity.
I will not give them the responsibility for my life.'

I hope these poems resonate for those who adopt and those who are adopted, but whatever our origins and wherever our lives take us, we all need to see, accept and parent the face we find in that mirror.

Blue Glass Empty Pram
From Exomphalos by Amy Goodrich: blue glass and light.

Powerfully silent.
A long wait come to nothing.

A low hum as white light
powers through a frail blue-glass skin,

searching like the thousand-eyed
operating theatre lamp.

I see it's shaped for a baby
but no wheels.

Icons of loss domesticate,
but this symbol,

cosy as a Semtex teddy,
offers no exit or entrance.

Lost Property

She's lost her memory.
Doesn't know where she put it –
keeps casting for its scent,
rattling cupboard doors.

Was it a hatbox or suitcase?
Which? Scuffed corners, cardboard
showing through, a bent brass key
on string?

Lost, lost; bus tickets, feathers,
hat-pins, a broken pen, an unstrung
necklace, her confirmation prayer book,
the vicar's spidery hand,
letter of reference from the cook,
her mother, hoping this finds her
as it leaves them at home.

No wedding lines.
A photo, bilious yellow as nicotine,
her on a stiff self-conscious khaki arm,
a black framed notice, creased,
some folded grey suede gloves.

Snippets of hats, she loved them. Petals
of artificial silk on blackened wire,
violets, peonies, roses, a liturgy of colour,
worn to church in hopes of rising
not again but now.

No passport either. A day return
to Scarborough. A weekend, later,
in Southend. She's lost it, lost it.

Under the pile, a birth certificate,
no father. A round dark head,
her breast a fountain choked too soon.

Doesn't know where she put it.
Knows it was a suitcase,
handle shaped for carrying.

She's lost her memory but not
its weight and shape and pain.

Well, Daughter...

hoping this, a line
aimed deeper
than a wrinkle in time,
finds you –
as it leaves me.

Never mind that you
weren't a plum coloured
bawling baby, braided
with birth blood,
a child, clean
as a new pinny,
rinsed with wind
from long-legged kites
walking the common,
a teenager, collecting
worldly smuts,
angles and pain,

somewhere you are –
on the other side
of a closed door.

Somewhere is the parcel
of birth pangs, broken nights,
wash-wrinkled hands,
measles, chicken-pox,
petulance, estrangement,
and painful love,
that belongs to me.

I am rich with its loss.
Absence creates
a room for echoes.

Deep in the mirror
of my own face
you look for me.

The French For Midwife

She is mourning her child
with a bitter green mourning,
stained as the distressed
liquor strained out before
his birth, all hard fruit
and black stone heart.

Her thighs and belly ache.
We have given her tea;
later we'll hand her baby,
wrapped like a present,
for her to hold.

We'll take his photograph
and send in the grief counsellor.
Yes, we'll say, deep eyed with wisdom,
you're bound to feel bitter.

Her husband has grown paws;
her skin thrums dangerously
at his touch. He'll go home
empty, get his mother
to pack up the baby clothes,
dig at the core of his pain
with a fistful of smoke
and a can of beer.

In the middle of the night
I ask myself,
what's the use of being a *sage femme*
if I can't help one
struggling new grief to be born.

Adoption

Bundle the orphaned lamb
in borrowed wool,
in the fresh warm skin
of one newly dead.
Restless, the ewe
smells her own blood
on a soft fleece
and lets down
the consolation
of her milk
to the small hard mouth
of a made-over lamb,
always printed for its mother
with another's feel and smell.

Sheep absorb puzzlement
like rain on sweet turf,
though their voices
when the lambs go
lace the spring sun
from a fog of separation.

Do you see me now
in my skin, in my own skin,
printed with relics
of a child never yours?

I will wear your echoes
for company, a sonar
in the foggy fields of death,
though they come back
sounding of my voice.

I will lay the skin
of my cheek against yours.

The Don't Touch Garden

'Mum, why don't I look like you?'
An age before freezers but my cucumber
and tinned salmon tinkle with ice.
Fresh from the bagwash, our Sunday cloth
becomes Siberian.

My father coughs the cough that kills
thirty years later. 'Not at the table, Jim...
And **you** eat up... good food... not for wasting...'
'But it's got bones, Mum.' Soft little blue-white
spicules, tasting of chalk. '**Eat.**' Safe, familiar
battleground, colluded victory. I eat,
we both pretend I'm filled.

Good food, a story hinted at, not told
for her. Bread and marge dipped in her Dad's
rich gravy. A gobstopper fluffed with lint,
scrumped apples, and once a pickled herring
up her drawers, nicked from the corner shop.

Later, she laid places,
footmen, garden boys, housemaids – and like
a massive liner coming over the rim
of daylight, Cook, for whom the bacon
must be shaven pink and curly, the egg's
golden eye shaded with a *Gloire de Dijon* lid.

Horn of plenty, blown for two and six
a month and one half day on which you went
to see your Mum, took her such leavings – jellied
dripping, windfalls, blown plums – as Cook
benignly sent '...all those children ... mouths to feed...
such a **respectable** woman, your mother...'

Panis angelicus. Is this the food of angels
or something else you've got to swallow down
and not get stuck or else you go to hell?

I'm s'posed to feel Him here. Welcome Jesus,
Sacred Heart, sorry for my sins...what else?
How long before He goes away?

The altar looks like meat, brown with yellow
curls. Don't think of liver, or you'll sick Him
up. The happiest day, they say

but I feel like a maypole with this soppy veil,
older than all the other waist-high kids, I had
to tell real sins to Father... Don't think about it

now with Jesus here, He'll listen in. O Mother
of the Word Incarnate, graciously
hear and answer me.

Not enough colour in her own red hair,
hips and haws, golden freckled chestnut leaves,
crimsons, gilded greens, the stained glass colours
of pantry, church and lane. Not hers to make
and touch, but lent, made-over, handed-down,
until my father came, his snappy trilby brim
forever cocked, always about to join his
raffish shadow to his own quiet soul.
Jews Harp, mouth organ, tapping foot,
beery voice of the pub, but Monday mornings
cancelled Saturday nights.

He'd give her a bit of life,
a place to call her own, a name,
he'd give her children.

Seven stains or clots.
The seventh breathed
awhile. The eighth,
a piece of paper.
Mum and Dad get happy-ever-after,
'a dear little Catholic baby girl'.

'She never sent her clothes – not
that I'd want them, hand-me-downs.
I threw out what she came in – shabby!
Navy blue eyes and scurf, she had
and crusts all round her eyes.
My sister Margaret said "*God*, Else!
You don't want that. Take it back."

How she cried. Her mouth
grazed past the rubber teat.
I tried to hold her close.
She snapped back like electric,
like I smelt all wrong.'

'Skinny, shrieking like a rabbit
snared. My hands so big. Nowhere to go

except for down the pub. Why did
she want one? Mine I'd understand

but this from nowhere. Blood will out,
they say. Our last one was a boy

all quiet and blue and still. My gut's
been hot and angry since that day.'

Cradle cap,
hot and angry, belly-button
tight as a frown, scalp
weeping, tear ducts not formed
for an avalanche of grief...
'I am the genie in the bottle of milk...
I shall smash it, burst
screaming out of my skin...'

'Oh... let her stop... PLEASE let her
stop... It's like she knows... I want her
perfect, mine... why won't her head heal up?
Why can't I feed her? I know my Jim
will make me take her back...'
No, he takes her in his hands,
hard as a wooden cradle
and rocks the rhythm of woe.

Skin our first sacrament

comes before water
on the other side of birth.

It is the last we long
to take on our tongues.

Between is waiting,
a long estrangement

bitterness, blundering
careless harm, lust.

Don't forgive me
my sharp-bladed back

mother, child, lover,
stranger to whom more

is due. Waiting is
a more exact return

until I offer my
simple skin to you.

'Come down two-legged'

my Dad invited, palm outstretched,
wooing. But the garden steps were

sharp as teeth and steep. Best to set
your bottom on the crumbling brick

wriggle, scrape, drop your short legs
and plop, safe to the next step. What

did he want? To catch me as I fell,
trust soft and heavy and solid

as a bag of sugar, or see me push
my legs out of my chrysalis and grow?

What did I want, caught between the top
step and the dizzy plunge of desire

or manipulation? Now citizen of two
cities, I know I need one serviceable leg

to follow the other over the fence
where I threw my heart

red as a tracer bullet and must
climb down at last.

'*Redyellerorraaange*!'

all run together
colours in the bagwash,
our words, the brightly
painted ball between tin paws
of a clockwork cat.

The key in its back slows.
Red, yellow, segments show.
My Dad can't wait to turn the key,
grabs the cat in his great fist,
arcs it round the floor.

He's in love with making
me laugh. Better than grimly
battled bottle and spoon,
his hunger, mine, dissolves
in fat chuckles, clockwork
colours, wild chants.

*Nib and Nob, A Tale of Two
Bad Mice, Rickety Rackety
Ramba, Bobby Bear* '...missed
a page, missed a page...' he can't
fool me. *I* know the code for words.

'Why do you hurt my Mummy
in the night? Why does she say
aah Jim?' His hands are still,
his ears red-rimmed. Their flaps
are closed. No words. Only
a retinal scribble, burning
where they've been.

Burning like a yew berry

in the sacred shaggy dark
churchyard tree, chosen

for its everlasting flame,
the flame of his everlasting

cigarette, his huge delicate
hands, things he wouldn't

things he couldn't say,
must put a match to,

steady red lantern,
fallen orange needle,

my blistered memory
cooled, now all his quietness

has become silence.

All the colour bled
suddenly from the day.
It had been haycock yellow
except in the green shadows
where hens tumbled their sleepy
vowels like sifted grain.

Roses, soft as creamy butter
on the back fence, delphiniums,
a tower of blue eyes fearlessly
gazing at the sky. No sirens. Me
in my new pink sun dress, my Mum
leaning against the shelter's hot
corrugated side, and birthday cake for tea.

'Else, Else... he's missing!'
Electric red hair squashed, a clippie hat,
half-moons of sweat, her grey summer
uniform acrid with grief. Aunty Bella,
likes a good time, now payment's due,
wrenches at the afternoon clock. Put
the hands back, don't let it happen! 'God.
I will be good... My Bert was good to me!'

'**Not** in front of her'. My mother
takes her arm. Moves her firmly down
the path. Their voices murmur. Bella's
rises, a sudden wild rain. *Shhhh!*
Nothing must be named. Too late.
Final as a siren or a bomb, marking
before and after, somewhere in France
and here, all the colour
has bled from the day.

There's something about a soldier,
something about a soldier...
'Your Uncle Bert's gone to be with
the angels. You mustn't be sad.' But
I'm not, though she's looking
in the mirror as she does my plaits
to see if I cry. Had I better?

Two pairs of brown eyes
crudely matched – hers tawny
lion bold, mine peat water –
glance off each other
in the quicksilver, waiting
to see who blinks first.

No good. Uncle Bert's
a composite, all the soldiers
in the street, hairy khaki, polished
pontoon boots, hard buttocks,
great hands, offering chocolate,
easing their belts, crotches
and vulnerable necks.

The angels are welcome. 'Now
Diane and Peter have got no Dad.'
Does she *want* me to cry? I can't!
Sidestep, quick! 'Did he kill lots
of Germans, Mum?'

Aunty Bella, my mother Molly,
and even Mum, who slides a look
when I'm not watching, know
something I'll never know,
something about a soldier that is fine
fine, fine...

D-Day coming. Even the stars blacked out.
Hanging like a small slow pendulum
on my father's arm. The North Circular
awash with the soft roar of trucks,
shimmering with the glowworm track
of cigarettes. White smiles at a kid
on the street, darkened faces.

Men, death, history.
No formulaic tears
to blur the blazing shape
of that archaic constellation.

'Come on! Let's go up the bomb-site
and play.' 'Can't. My Mum says I mustn't,
s'dangerous...' ' Cowardy cowardy custard, dip yer
nose in mustard!' It's inside out. In graceful swatches

forget-me-not faded bedroom paper facing
the street. Bath in the cellar – never was a cellar
when the house was whole. Somebody died

in it when the bomb fell, they say. Blood or rust
under its green taps? What shall we play?
Cowboys? No, you need asphalt to gallop
your horse. Cops and robbers? Too scary.
Still smell of burning and a faint skittering
sift of falling plaster dust or elder leaves,
brushes your nerves. Springy mattress
of fireweed covering ash. Mothers and Fathers?

Early in the morning I once saw
my mother's bush blazing in the shadow
of her moonlit thighs. 'Bless me Father,
for I have sinned,' who have yet to learn
how sin is never what you want,
only what you do, and often don't.
How flesh jerks away from giving kindness.

How starve and chill takes longer
to kill, but is as sure as fire.

Mr Lip,
Lippingwell, actually, used to paint a duck egg
for me every Easter with my hated name,
and as he was a coach painter it had gilded
curlicues, rich arabesques of gold on crimson,
but still I didn't like it. It said 'Kathleen.'

He had a nervous leg. Used to sit in his carver,
smoke like dense blue ectoplasm coughing
out of his bitten pipe, one leg tapping, waiting
for his chops to burn. My Mum used to let him
watch me play in the bath. I didn't like that, either.

Mrs Lip smelled like a damp tea towel. Older
than him, she made *my Charlie* mahogany tea,
and every night burned his meat black with loving
panic.
'He'll leave me, Else.' She'd call my Mum downstairs
and cry. I wished he would. His leg twitched when he
looked at me.

Kathleen

quivering like a hazel twig, how can I
love you now you've lost your name?

It had to go. 'I'll take you
HOME again Kathleeeen'

roared from the pub, rich
round mock Irish vowels

mellow as malt, swooping
like a drunken budgie,

where you stood, loving
the clean rain. 'To where

your heart has EVER BEEN...'
Losing your name

a small necessary mutilation
to find who? Me, who can't wean

myself from a small shudder
at the sound of your name, *Kathleen*?

At last I know my name

not how I was called into this flesh,
blackberry bundle of cells
priested by my mother

whose only vestments, the long
aisles of blood, chanted 'stay'
when she meant to say 'go!'

Yellow, fragile, bound up in cliché
and elastic bands, found under
lisle stockings and knickers,

my pre-history, partial as all true
stories, her name, solid as bread
in my gullet, mine

fragile at first in my mouth so
I fear the room, smelling of dust
and afternoon and old bedclothes

will swallow it, but I say it and taste
only the clean iron-smelling rain

Fragments preserved.

A bronze smile,
a pot belly, curved as buttocks,
a clipped coin.

Where is the context
for a smile without a face
an empty pot, a crime
now long forgotten?

Other significant things

some buried, some archived
as if they were meant to be
visited in the dusty stack.

Fresh as plain paper
the smell of kindness
lacerates. You

taught me how images
cohere and one face
gathers them. Now

older or more knowing,
when grief

aches like a funnybone
I honour the wise ambiguity
of fragments.

When I took my Mum
to the Folk Museum
she fingered the washing-
dolly lightly, though you
shouldn't touch.

Splintered, roughed-up
by soda, it stood near granular black
cast-iron smoothing irons,

a copper, clumsy wooden tongs,
a zinc tub and pegs, bound
with tin strips, from gypsies
who hung their wash on hawthorns.

A room still smelling faintly
of steam and wet aprons
but the roil and bash
of wash day quiet now.

She read the label. 'O, my back!
They don't say that...'

Later I found her in the don't
touch garden, stolen cuttings
sticking from her handbag,
face to the late sun.

Milk

She never smelt of milk.
Sweat and sometimes fear
crackled like burnt paper
behind her overall –

when the doodle-bug's clock-work
stopped, quiet as a feather
and she crammed my face
into butchers sawdust,
pine and greasy blood,

when I coughed
or wouldn't coax
cold gobs of cod
into my mouth
squared off to cry,

when in my new stilettoes
and sugar starched slip,
creaking like ice,
I limped home
after midnight,

when my father, twisting
in the smoke of pain,
refused to die
until she said the word,
crossly, at last,

when lavender soap,
clean sheets, stale air
and disinfectant replacing sweat,
she stared down death
like jack in its box,

but worst, when her breasts ached,
I roared, the landlady tutted,
my borrowed father sighed,
she never smelt of milk.

Elephant Aunts

My Aunt only knew the title,
my best book,
the one I begged for every night,
not that I called her Elephant Aunt
because her legs, stout and shapeless,
armchair thighs, bun feet,
recalled the Aunts' comfortable
grey, wrinkled ankles.

Wholly benign,
the Elephant Aunts.
Sisters. One wore spectacles.
Both had kind little
piggy eyes. You knew
their trunks would soothe,
like cool wet velvet,
tip to nape.

My Aunt, though...
Once in a draper's
I saw a bolt of flannel
bound down the mahogany
counter like a heifer,
dangerous run-away cloth.
You might long
for the wise upholstery
of a lap. You got cake
and its consequences.

Planted. Not a word I knew,
but the Elephant Aunts' legs
thrust up, carrying the weight
of their great grey bellies and their
flowered pinnies, while rooting
them in jungle earth.

Set, my Aunt was, I
learned later, though
more like blancmange
than concrete. How
the Elephant Aunts
would have dignified
my bones with kisses,
a child not theirs,

owning only the short-sighted
kindness of their clever hearts,
not bothering about *blood
will out.* Lucky I believed
in them first, vast grey
benignancies, in my father's
bed-time voice,

before I learned that *thicker
than water* hissed at the tea table
wasn't a cup of weak tea,
but how you described
who I would never be.

The Man on a Bike

'Tell me! What did he say…?'

She means 'What did he *do*?'
She'll ask me soon, but I won't say.

Coals shift in our tiny grate,
little blue hisses, sulphurous farts,
smell like wet horses.

I'm standing in a chipped enamel bowl,
water gone cold and scummy,
red sliver of Lifebuoy, an extra finger
poking as she scrubs a little harder.

'You'll have to say if you saw him,
the policeman wants to know.'
She soaps between my legs so hard
my buttocks set
like bannister knobs.

'Course I won't tell her,
she smacked my bum only for taking
sixpence from Uncle Ted,
silly old man on a bicycle's worth
more than a slap, I expect.

How did he hold his bike so still,
one hand on the sit-up-and-beg handlebars,
the other tenting his long mac,
hem draggling its chain,
poised on two wheels
like a wave waiting to fall,
his little purple thing
less naked than his face?

Our clock ticks, its sturdy
oak overcoat humming,
before the next strike.

'Six o'clock. Your Dad'll
make you tell.' Minutes stretch,
frail as unbroken Yankee chewing gum.
I make my eyes opaque as chocolate.

Bedtime at last.

Trust me
He doesn't say it, words are scarce.
On ration. Makes soft little mumbles,
nudges with his voice, furrows
his freckled forehead, its white band
where his trilby sits.

Dong – quarter past six, he's missed his news.
Must be important. Hasn't had his tea.
A gilded rim round the soft, washed out
blur of our bedroom curtains. Bird cries
of kids in the street. Daylight out there.

Wants me to say, something, anything,
not too much, my mother's shadow
twisting its hands on the landing. 'He didn't...?'
This I can do. 'No, Dad.' Their bed, its muffled cave
of sighs and groans you're not supposed to hear

gives me the clue. 'I didn't see anything.'
Eyes soft and grateful he tucks me in
his hard hands sheathed.

My mother thrums, neglected steam,
she knows I am my Daddy's girl,
while she, guardian of the grit
in our family gizzard,
grinds different stones.

Mothers and Fathers

A very wise poet once said lovers
'are each other's parents'.

I don't think you're my father,
that puzzled, gentle, blunt-handed

man. Maybe you occupy the space
where touch might have been skin

and feeding nurture? Your
hands smell of leaves, compost

and piano keys.
Time to play

mothers and fathers again,
to say 'table' and 'bed'

and 'house' but mothered
and fathered at last,

let the roof shelter
nouns into verbs.

The Cot of my Bones our Bed

The cot of my bones
carries a child life;
running between bars,
down our endless street,
fast footprints, past bedtime,
she escapes in shrill bird-cries.

She is under the bobble-fringed
table, behind a chair,
sliding from the green mirror.
I never see her face.

Closest in night's core,
I feel her breath on my cheek,
feel astronaut-light;
my body, an ache delivered;
her live weight now moving
in the dark outside.

Does she have
an alphabet frock,
scabbed knees?

Will she forgive me?
My cheeks stained
by feral nights,
ghosts humping
frantic sheets,
ears naked
in a byre of sounds.

She's born now,
sulky-mouthed,
limp-curled,
smelling of secretive
child sweat, boiled sweets,
and fragrant pencil wood
chewed in dumb patience.

I follow her
down the long, moving
mirror curve and lean
my grown-up face
over her sharp
turned back.

Corchipoo

'Corchipoo' growls my mother,
snuffling bearlike
into my neck. 'Corchipoo,'
her word for snoring.

Still sunlight, chips of amber,
blips on brown Anaglypta.
Me in the fat armchair;
its smell of bottoms
and cigarettes; strands
of yarn combed over
its bald spots.

She means 'go to sleep',
but kindly. We've played
feetupthewall and butterfly
kisses, so it's ok, curled up
on the uncut moquette
to let go the daylight
clamped in my fists.

If I dream of lions
they'll bounce on the balls
of their paws,
red and laughing
like my chestnut Mum.

'Corchipoo.' At night
it sounds so different;
thin, with an edge.
Roll up tight and pretend.
If my eyelashes quiver
I'll get a wallop.

Why does the magic
mask of dark
blot out her amber,
leave just the heat of her hand?

Sometimes they purr;
two slumbrous great
bees, corchipoo, corchipoo.
Then their big bed is anchored.
It's safe to let the thin
dark stuff of night
trickle from my wrists.

But when their bed
breaks loose, bucks
on a torrent of sound,
my ears scrape back,
I scrabble to hold on.

Two black boulders,
they roll apart, groan
and settle... corchipoo.

Soft silt of sleep
shoals up our room.

I wait. Slowly
the tide of dark
bleaches. When
it turns I sleep.

Thyrotoxicosis

Under her size eighteen
I'd always suspected a witch.
Sure enough, she melted down.

Had I really done it?
My mother burned like a stick.
She blamed me. Her hands
clattered the pots
like chattering teeth.
Bolting around the kitchen
her eyes panicked,
hunting down why.

I'd always known
she didn't smell right;
they'd stolen me.

When I saw her, in perfect sheets,
quiet as a whisper, her deer's eyes
skittering mildly on white walls,
a white bandage on her throat,
I choked. My shaken flesh
leaned towards hers.
She tried to smile. I cried.
Ostermilk was thicker than blood.

My Father, Counting Sheep

He has been awake
for long enough, counting.
His life is thick, painful
seconds, squeezed from the glass.

Stretching his eyes behind
the sharp sun's lance
he waits
for the terrible medicine of dark.

He has his mother's eyes.
Often she rapped his head
with bony knuckles,
her fierce hazel glint
searching out sin like truffles.

She never cured him of looking;
silk in the rag bag,
silver in clouds.

Now, his rib cage winnowed
with scorching breath,
his big glove puppet hands
tell their own story
to the sheets.

Somewhere in the dry
fields of his brain
he is driving his last
ragged thoughts relentlessly,
over and over,
past the same gate,
counting to keep awake.

What gives him quiet?
Not me with my bolus
of love and drugs.
My mother, her voice
shrill with familiar strain,
whispers angrily tender,
'let GO!' He sighs.
His flocks line up soberly.
All the mild sheep
are folded through his eyes.

Sometimes I Feel Another Face

known but unknown,
settling on me like light rain.

I'm tempted to wear it,
to choose, not as I was chosen,
a random button
from my mother's button box,
though each one had its story,
a scrap of whole cloth
dangling from its shank.

My mother murdered cabbage.
It died with a yelp in the pot.
My *in memoriam* for her smells
of crushed red pepper, slightly charred,
sweet garlic and a sexy golden
lick of olive oil, soft as lamplight.

Can I swear to kill no more vegetables,
leave out soda and scarifying salt,
unpick the sampler, edged with piggy
little brussel sprouts, white sugar,
iron pie-crusts, tea to trot a mouse on,
ignore the poker-work plaque, instructing
Bisto, tinned marrow-fat peas,
and yet be daughter?

Worse, none of my china will match
and I shall go to bed naked every night
snug in the duvet of a lover's breast
who is not of my tribe.

I will trace her face
in the separate dark and afterwards,
mine, growing at last its own trembling
possibility of nakedness.

Making the Days

It is like waving off a train,
Small and peaky, growing smaller
your face is burrowed in its chins.
Cheek skin runnelled,
old laugh lines like scars
till they flesh up firm
when you grin.

Each last bit,
a casual photo at a church fete,
an outing to the coast –
too far to go again
your breath too raw –
is another telegraph pole
flashing past on the rackety line,
beating out the journey
with gathering tempo.

You never wanted to stop
or get off,
rather let the Christmas treat
merge with a doze in your chair.

How will you rest?
God was never responsible
for the green spears in your garden,
your profligate house plants,
or even the swallows
skimming ripe barley.

You made the world
seven times over each day
between breakfast and tea,
and peopled it,
a touch of iron
for those who strayed
beyond the picket
of your imagination.

It may be more of a day trip
than a journey, a dignity
of simply going with the wheels,
too tired to keep on
making the days.

The End of a Long Conversation has Come

I zip you inside the fat purse of memory
along with hairpins, old bus tickets, creased, velvety
as suede, heavy coppers and soft, face-powder dust.

I have collected all our tears in a small bottle
and put it on the shelf with the household gods
in the kitchen where you might hear the pots chatter
in a foreign lingo – ***garlic*?*?**

I've shelved our conversations – were they ever? – or
more than a way of filling the silence,
were they you overwriting my memory with yours?
Either way, the brown spools are packed in plastic cassettes.

All the black and white photographs, their ghosts,
the shadows of faces just out of shot, the long darkening
in front of the one behind the shutter, lie collated,
in a tin trunk, rustling with the DNA of years.

I have broken the record. The one that asks
did you mean it? Did I? Sometimes
fragments speak the truth
and broken is better than whole.

Now I button you, curiously small
but safe in your own dignity
in my inside pocket.
We never did say goodbye.

Oral History

My mother's story
skimmed blue as milk

rounds no stones in buried watercourses
deposits no shattered teacups

is breath
and as breath
grows thin and fitful no longer equal to the task
of story
scattering the small hard seed of consonants and vowels.

The ponderous gold grille of the bakelite
wireless sieved
fragments and static foreign as semaphore.

Where do the words go?
Up in Annie's room behind the clock she said.
Let me tell it I'd say.
You weren't there she'd answer as if there was a time
when I was not.

Now I must go quietly and cannily as an evening fox
carrying my wounded bundle of news
in my careful mouth.

On Growing a Face
for my biological mother

Broad-bean sized I clung on.
You swigged gin, boiled your flesh, fell off your chair,
        yet I've been half in love with you all my life.
Fed regular shots of bitter-as-vodka adrenaline, I learned
to spot a nun's voice, cutting through womb-walls,
        to cling harder, root for you, *in* you,
head over heels, tumbling on my string, while your hands,
scrubbed, bleached, and cracked, blushed red,
        as you, too proud, would never do.

While I was growing your face, not knowing
I'd only ever see it backwards, in the mirror,
        not seeing was believing –
you planned to lose your long-term, live-in lover
as I grew helpless little nubs of love
        like extra digits.
I learned that love's
a climbing frame for separation, teaches
        gaps and leaps and reaches.

Now my own face has grown – and yours has peeled away
from friends and lovers where you always hid,
        just out of sight –
I light a candle in that space
where voice and face and grace
        and muscle of absence grow.

The Right Bones

'Where do birds usually go to die?' you ask.
'Is there somewhere like an elephants graveyard?'

A passing car or cat got this one.
Its down jacket must still be warm.

Quills are oil-slick bright, upstanding
but its ruby eyes are dull little gravels

and its coral feet a crippled grey.
Somebody, imitating the reticent

decency of the way birds like to die
has swept it into a doorway.

I imagine a bird feeling its pulse fail,
settling its last warmth

on the I Ching puzzle of its ancestors bones
folding the wings it won't need

round the small leaves of its feet,
quietly letting the migratory knot

in its forehead fade.
I would like that too

one day
if only I can find the right bones.

Oma

I'm my own grandmother.
How? I'm no believer

but every time I open my door
and pass those two caryatids, Love and Kindness

standing in the hall, I touch their worn
marble hems prayerfully.

Where I once failed to love my mirror,
now I see light and threads the Norns have spun,

or might – a canny harvesting of sun,
a shine from other faces, shadow,

a leading dark that stitches me
my proper place.

Mothers? I've put them to bed with my dolls,
but more tenderly, older and gentler now,

still in need of my own forgiveness
though not of theirs. And the child?

Harder. Some children have such very old, small faces
shrink-wrapped in sorrow.

Only the grandmother of time
can lay a finger on their cheeks.

Bison

Only a cold, acrid stink as my boot
crushes its dung in wet grass.

Empty horizons. Skies herding great flocks
of thunderheads. Plains still as a mirror

that swallows my reflection
and refuses to give it back.

At the outside edge of the limit of vision
a puff of dust kicked up by a disappearing hoof.

My prehistory is blank as a people without pots
or bones. I won't find the warm flank

of a live bison so I'll touch the ribs,
caging my own heart first; then perhaps, gently

with the living tips of my fingers,
I could feel yours.

Paradox

'Mirror, mirror on the wall'
the old joke says
'I am my mother after all'

but which?

Feathers, grain, eggs, fluff.
I had two mothers once.
More than enough.

A red hen and a white,
two mothers once.
One stayed and one took flight.

The red laid eggs that broke.
The white flew off
to avoid the yoke.

Not before time in grace
of mirror light a third appears.
Late and slow I learn her face.

Feathers, grain, eggs, fluff.
Three mothers now.
More than enough.

MORE FROM ARACHNE PRESS
www.arachnepress.com

BOOKS

London Lies ISBN: 978-1-909208-00-1
Our first Liars' League showcase, featuring unlikely tales set in London.

Stations ISBN: 978-1-909208-01-8
A story for every station from New Cross, Crystal Palace, and West Croydon at the Southern extremes of the Overground line all the way to Highbury & Islington.

Lovers' Lies ISBN: 978-1-909208-02-5
Our second collaboration with Liars' League, bringing the freshness, wit, imagination and passion of their authors to stories of love.

Weird Lies ISBN: 978-1-909208-10-0
WINNER of the Saboteur2014 Best Anthology Award: our third Liars' League collaboration – more than twenty stories varying in style from tales not out of place in *One Thousand and One Nights* to the completely bemusing.

Mosaic of Air, Cherry Potts ISBN: 978-1-909208-03-2
Sixteen short stories from a lesbian perspective.

Devilskein & Dearlove, Alex Smith ISBN: 978-1-909208-15-5
Nominated for the 2015 CILIP Carnegie Medal.
Young Erin Dearlove has lost everything, and is living in a run-down apartment block in Cape Town. Then she has tea with Mr Devilskein, the demon who lives on the top floor, and opens a door into another world.

The Other Side of Sleep: Narrative Poems
ISBN: 978-1-909208-18-6
Long, narrative poems by contemporary voices, including Inua Elams, Brian Johnstone, and Kate Foley, whose title poem for the anthology was the winner of the 2014 *Second Light* Long Poem competition.

Solstice Shorts: Sixteen Stories about Time
ISBN: 978-1-909208-23-0
Winning stories from the first Solstice Shorts Festival competition together with a story from each of the competition judges.

All our books (except *The Other Side of Sleep* and *The Don't Touch Garden*) are also available as e-books.

EVENTS

Arachne Press is enthusiastic about live literature and we make an effort to present our books through readings. We showcase our work and that of others at our own bi-monthly live literature event in south London: *The Story Sessions*, which we run like a folk club, with headliners and opportunities for the audience to join in (http://arachnepress.com/the-story-sessions/); and we ran our first all-day festival, Solstice Shorts (http://arachnepress.com/solstice-shorts/), in December 2015; but we are always on the lookout for other places to show off, so if you run a bookshop, a literature festival or any other kind of literature venue, get in touch, we'd love to talk to you.

WORKSHOPS

We offer writing workshops, suitable for writers' groups, literature festivals, evening classes – if you are interested, please let us know.

follow us on twitter @arachnepress
like us on Facebook https://www.facebook.com/ArachnePress

MORE ABOUT KATE FOLEY

An extended video interview between Kate Foley and editor Cherry Potts about the events behind these poems is available at http://arachnepress.com/poets/kate-foley/

Like Kate on Facebook
https://www.facebook.com/pages/Kate-Foley/1429010410739779